MILITARY AIRCRAFT
B-52 STRATOFORTRESS
BY JOHN HAMILTON

VISIT US AT
WWW.ABDOPUBLISHING.COM

Published by ABDO Publishing Company, PO Box 398166, Minneapolis, MN 55439.
Copyright ©2013 by Abdo Consulting Group, Inc. International copyrights reserved in all
countries. No part of this book may be reproduced in any form without written permission
from the publisher. A&D Xtreme™ is a trademark and logo of ABDO Publishing Company.

Printed in the United States of America, North Mankato, Minnesota.
102012
012013

Editor: Sue Hamilton
Graphic Design: Sue Hamilton
Cover Design: John Hamilton
Cover Photo: U.S. Air Force
Interior Photos: All photos United States Air Force except: Getty-pgs 26-27; United
States Army-pg 18; United States Navy-pgs 28-29.

ABDO Booklinks
Web sites about Military Aircraft are featured on our Book Links pages. These links
are routinely monitored and updated to provide the most current information available.
Web site: www.abdopublishing.com

Cataloging-in-Publication Data

Hamilton, John, 1959-
 B-52 Stratofortress / John Hamilton.
    p. cm. -- (Xtreme military aircraft set 2)
Includes index.
ISBN 978-1-61783-687-9
1. B-52 bombers--Juvenile literature. 2. Airplanes, Military--United States--
Juvenile literature. I. Title.
623.74--dc15
                    2012945706

TABLE OF CONTENTS

B-52 Stratofortress 4

Origins. 6

Upgrades 8

Mission: Strategic Bombing 10

Mission: Close Air Support 12

B-52 Stratofortress Fast Facts 14

Airframe. 16

Engines 18

Range 20

Weapons 22

Crew 24

Combat History 26

The Future 28

Glossary. 30

Index 32

B-52 ★★★
STRATOFORTRESS

The B-52 Stratofortress is a long-range, heavy bomber. It is flown by the United States Air Force. It has been flown since the 1950s. It is regularly modernized and upgraded. The B-52 flies many kinds of missions. It can even carry the most destructive weapons of all: nuclear bombs.

"Stratofortress" roughly means "fortress in the clouds." The B-52 is more commonly nicknamed "BUFF" (Big Ugly Fat Fellow).

A U.S. Air Force B-52 Stratofortress bomber flies a mission over the Pacific Ocean in July 2010.

ORIGINS

The first version of the B-52 was the B-52A. It first flew in 1954. The plane's manufacturer, Boeing, tested the plane and modified it. The B-52B entered service with the United States Air Force in 1955.

B-52s played an important role during the Cold War period from the 1950s to 1991. The planes were loaded with nuclear bombs. It was hoped this would prevent, or deter, the Soviet Union or other enemies from attacking the United States.

XTREME FACT

During the Cold War, many B-52s flew near the Soviet Union's border. This ensured a rapid strike in case of a Soviet nuclear attack.

UPGRADES

A total of 744 B-52s were built for the United States Air Force. The latest version is the B-52H. It is the only version still flying today.

XTREME FACT

The current fleet of B-52s is expected to last at least until 2040.

Over the years, the aircraft has been continuously upgraded. It now has advanced flight controls, navigation aids, and better weapons. Even though the aircraft's design is over 60 years old, the B-52 performs better today than when it was new.

An armed B-52H Stratofortress flies over Afghanistan in 2006.

MISSION: STRATEGIC BOMBING

When it first entered service, the B-52's main mission was strategic bombing.

A B-52 drops a load of M-117 bombs in Iraq during Operation Desert Storm.

A strategic bomber is big enough to fly long distances and carry heavy loads of bombs. It is not used on the battlefield to support friendly troops. Instead, a strategic bomber flies deep into enemy territory and destroys military bases, roads, factories, even whole cities.

XTREME FACT

The Air Force today flies three strategic bombers: the B-52, the B-1B Lancer, and the B-2 Spirit.

MISSION: CLOSE AIR SUPPORT

One of the B-52's biggest strengths is that it is a flexible weapons platform. It can perform many kinds of missions. After the Cold War ended in the 1990s, many B-52s were converted to perform close air support missions. Close air support means helping friendly forces in the battle zone. The B-52 can carry smart bombs that strike the enemy even when close to friendly forces. The aircraft can also fly at night or in poor weather.

An airman performs a weapons loading check under the wing of a B-52H Stratofortress in 2012.

XTREME FACT

Although originally intended to fly at high altitude, many B-52s now fly combat missions at low altitude to evade enemy radar.

B-52 STRATOFORTRESS FAST FACTS

The B-52 can fly day or night, and can be refueled in the air. The only range limitation is the ability of the crew to stay awake and alert after many hours in the air.

B-52 Stratofortress Specifications

Function:	Heavy Bomber
Service Branch:	United States Air Force
Manufacturer:	Boeing
Length:	159 feet, 4 inches (48.6 m)
Height:	40 feet, 8 inches (12.4 m)
Wingspan:	185 feet (56.4 m)
Crew:	5
Speed:	650 miles per hour (1,046 kph)
Range:	8,800 miles (14,162 km)
Ceiling:	50,000 feet (15,240 m)

AIRFRAME

The B-52 is a huge, unusual-looking aircraft. Its wingspan is 185 feet (56.4 m), more than half the length of a football field. The wings are swept backwards, which keeps the aircraft more stable at its top speed of 650 miles per hour (1,046 kph). B-52s are tough aircraft. They can fly safely even when heavily damaged.

XTREME FACT

In 1964, a B-52 test flight resulted in the entire vertical stabilizer, or tail fin, ripping off. Despite the damage, the aircraft returned safely.

A B-52 Stratofortress moves off after an aerial refueling.

ENGINES

Each B-52 is powered by eight Pratt & Whitney TF33 turbofan engines. There are four engine pods, each containing a pair of engines. There are two pods on each wing. The B-52 needs this tremendous power so it can lift heavy loads of bombs and other cargo. However, if an engine is damaged or flames out, the bomber can easily return safely using the remaining engines.

Engine Pods

Engine Pods

A B-52 has four engine pods, each containing a pair of engines for a total of eight engines.

Airmen maintain a B-52's engine at Barksdale Air Force Base in Louisiana.

XTREME FACT

When taking off, the B-52's eight engines make a deafening roar that can be heard for many miles.

RANGE

The B-52 is a strategic bomber. That means it is built to fly long distances to strike deep inside enemy territory. A B-52 can fly 8,800 miles (14,162 km) before refueling. With mid-air refueling, the bomber's range is limited only by the stamina of the crew.

In 1996, during Operation Desert Strike, two B-52s struck Baghdad, Iraq, from their base at Barksdale Air Force Base, Louisiana. The 16,000-mile (25,750-km) round-trip mission took 34 hours to complete. It was one of the longest combat missions ever flown.

A B-52 Stratofortress is refueled by a KC-135 Stratotanker in the air over the Indian Ocean.

WEAPONS

The B-52 can carry almost every weapon the U.S. Air Force uses. These include nuclear bombs, cruise missiles, normal gravity bombs, GPS- or laser-guided "smart bombs," or even sea mines. The B-52 finds its targets using a combination of GPS, radar, or laser targeting systems. With the newly deployed Litening II laser targeting pod, the B-52 can even attack moving ground targets.

An airman inspects a B-52's Litening II laser targeting pod.

Most of the B-52's weapons are stored in its bomb bay, inside the cavernous fuselage. The B-52 can also carry bombs or cruise missiles under its wings.

Bombs are loaded onto a B-52 Stratofortress.

XTREME FACT

The B-52 can carry a payload (carrying capacity) of up to 70,000 pounds (31,751 kg) of weapons.

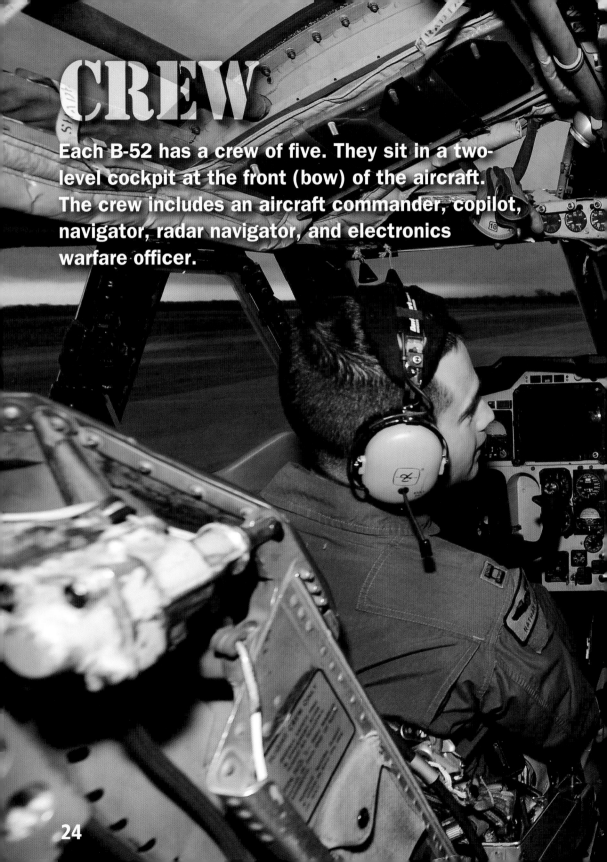

CREW

Each B-52 has a crew of five. They sit in a two-level cockpit at the front (bow) of the aircraft. The crew includes an aircraft commander, copilot, navigator, radar navigator, and electronics warfare officer.

In the past, only men flew on B-52s. Today, each job is filled by both male and female aircrew members.

XTREME FACT

Early versions of the B-52 included a tail gunner who manned powerful machine guns in the rear of the plane.

COMBAT HISTORY

B-52s carried nuclear weapons during the Cold War. The purpose was to prevent, or deter, the Soviet Union from attacking the United States. Thankfully, these weapons were never used.

B-52s dropping non-nuclear bombs have been used in many conflicts. During the Vietnam War of the 1960s and 1970s, B-52s were used to carpet bomb enemy bases.

A B-52 drops a load of bombs onto enemy positions in 1968 during the Vietnam War.

In 1991, B-52s destroyed many enemy targets during Operation Desert Storm in Kuwait and Iraq. B-52s were also used in the 2000s during Operation Enduring Freedom in Afghanistan, and during Operation Iraqi Freedom in Iraq.

THE FUTURE

The United States Air Force's fleet of B-52s is continually upgraded and refurbished. New electronics and reinforced parts greatly extend the aircrafts' service life. The Air Force expects to fly B-52s at least until 2040 or later.

A B-52 Stratofortress bomber flanked by two U.S. Navy F/A-18 Hornets fly past the USS Nimitz *aircraft carrier near Guam.*

Eventually, B-52s will have to be replaced. The stress of high-speed, low-altitude flight on the bombers' wings will someday make them unsafe. The Air Force is currently working on a new generation of long-range bombers. It may use stealth technology, like the current B-2 Spirit bomber. Some versions may also be unmanned.

GLOSSARY

CARPET BOMB

To bomb a small area, such as a military base or city, with an overwhelming amount of explosives, with the intent of completely covering, or "carpeting," the area with destruction.

COLD WAR

The Cold War was a time of political, economic, and cultural tension between the United States and its allies and the Soviet Union and other Communist nations. It lasted from about 1947, just after the end of World War II, until the early 1990s, when the Soviet Union collapsed and Communism was no longer a major threat to the United States.

ELECTRONICS WARFARE OFFICER

Responsible for defending the aircraft against enemy threats. The electronics warfare officer monitors sensors to check for enemy missiles or aircraft. If a threat is imminent, the officer can release chaff or flares, or jam enemy radar.

GPS (GLOBAL POSITIONING SYSTEM)

A system of orbiting satellites that transmits information to GPS receivers on Earth. Using information from the satellites, receivers can calculate location, speed, and direction with great accuracy.

OPERATION DESERT STORM

Also known as the Persian Gulf War (or simply the Gulf War). A war fought from 1990-1991 in Iraq and Kuwait between the forces of Iraq's President Saddam Hussein and a group of United Nations countries led by the United States.

RADAR

A way to detect objects, such as aircraft or ships, using electromagnetic (radio) waves. Radar waves are sent out by large dishes, or antennas, and then strike an object. The radar dish then detects the reflected wave, which can tell operators how big an object is, how fast it is moving, its altitude, and its direction.

SMART BOMB

Precision-guided weapons, also called "smart bombs," are bombs or missiles that can be steered in mid-air toward their targets. They are guided by lasers, radar, or satellite signals.

TURBOFAN ENGINE

A jet engine that receives an additional boost from a turbine-driven fan. Also called a fanjet.

VIETNAM WAR

A conflict between the countries of North Vietnam and South Vietnam from 1955-1975. Communist North Vietnam was supported by China and the Soviet Union. The United States entered the war on the side of South Vietnam.

INDEX

A

Afghanistan 9, 27
Air Force, U.S. 4, 5, 6, 8, 11, 15, 22, 28, 29

B

B-1B Lancer 11
B-2 Spirit 11, 29
Baghdad, Iraq 20
Barksdale Air Force Base 19, 20
Boeing 6, 15
BUFF (Big Ugly Fat Fellow) 5

C

Cold War 7, 12, 26

E

engine pods 18

F

F/A-18 Hornet 28

G

GPS (Global Positioning System) 22
Guam 28

H

Hornet (*see* F/A-18 Hornet)

I

Indian Ocean 21
Iraq 11, 20, 27

K

KC-135 Stratotanker 21
Kuwait 27

L

Lancer (*see* B-1B Lancer)
Litening II laser targeting pod 22
Louisiana 19, 20

N

Navy, U.S. 28
Nimitz, USS 28

O

Operation Desert Storm 10, 27
Operation Desert Strike 20
Operation Enduring Freedom 27
Operation Iraqi Freedom 27

P

Pacific Ocean 5
Pratt & Whitney 18

R

radar 13, 22

S

Soviet Union 7, 26
Spirit (*see* B-2 Spirit)
Stratotanker (*see* KC-135 Stratotanker)

T

TF33 turbofan engines 18

U

United States 4, 5, 6, 7, 8, 15, 22, 26, 28

V

Vietnam War 26, 27